ELVIS PRESLEY

By Adele Q. Brown

WORLD ALMANAC® LIBRARY

Please visit our web site at: www.worldalmanaclibrary.com
For a free color catalog describing World Almanac® Library's list
of high-quality books and multimedia programs, call 1-800-848-2928 (USA)
or 1-800-387-3178 (Canada). World Almanac® Library's fax: (414) 332-3567.

Library of Congress Cataloging-in-Publication Data

Brown, Adele Q.
    Elvis Presley / by Adele Q. Brown.
        p. cm. — (Trailblazers of the modern world)
    Includes bibliographical references and index.
    Summary: Follows the life, career, and music of the popular rock and roll singer, from his early years in Mississippi
to his controversial death at age forty-two.
    ISBN 0-8368-5085-8 (lib. bdg.)
    ISBN 0-8368-5245-1 (softcover)
    1. Presley, Elvis, 1935-1977—Juvenile literature. 2. Rock musicians—United States—Biography—Juvenile
literature. [1. Presley, Elvis, 1935-1977. 2. Singers. 3. Rock music.] I. Title. II. Series.
ML3930.P73B76   2003
782.42166'092—dc21
[B]   2002034303

First published in 2003 by
World Almanac® Library
330 West Olive Street, Suite 100
Milwaukee, WI 53212 USA

Copyright © 2003 by World Almanac® Library.

Project manager: Jonny Brown
Editor: Betsy Rasmussen
Design and page production: Scott M. Krall
Photo research: Diane Laska-Swanke
Indexer: Walter Kronenberg

Photo credits: © AP/Wide World Photos: 7 both, 12, 13 bottom, 16 top, 18 bottom, 22 top, 24, 33, 35, 36, 38;
© Bettmann/CORBIS: 8, 13 top, 14 bottom, 16 bottom, 19, 23, 25 both, 26, 34, 43; © Tami Chappell/Reuters/Getty
Images: 40; © CORBIS SYGMA: 42; © Richard Ellis/Getty Images: 41; Elvis images used by permission, Elvis Presley
Enterprises, Inc.: 21 bottom, 39; © Getty Images: 14 top; © Hulton Archive: cover, 4, 5 both, 11, 17, 18 top, 22 bottom,
27, 29; Photofest: 21 top; © Mario Tama/Getty Images: 37

Printed in the United States of America

1 2 3 4 5 6 7 8 9 07 06 05 04 03

TABLE of CONTENTS

Words that appear in the glossary are printed in **boldface** type the first time they occur in the text.

CHAPTER 1

"THE KING OF ROCK 'N' ROLL"

In addition to his musical ability, it's easy to see how Elvis Presley's casual good looks helped capture the hearts of teenagers in 1955.

Elvis Presley was not the first person to sing **rock 'n' roll**, but he was one of the most influential. Often called "The King of Rock 'n' Roll" or just "The King," he lit the world of popular music on fire, and he kept that fire burning for many years.

It all began in 1956, when Elvis blasted onto the scene with his first hit, "Heartbreak Hotel." From then until his death in 1977, he was a giant in the music field—a superstar. And even though there have been many superstars since Elvis, none has come close to topping the charts as often as he did. With 107 Top Forty hits, 38 Top Ten hits, and 10 consecutive hits that reached number one, his statistics leave everyone else in the dust.

One reason Elvis topped the charts so often is that he appealed to different audiences. His records were hits on the pop charts, the **rhythm and blues (R&B)** charts, and the country charts—sometimes, all at the same time. Few singers before or since can claim such widespread appeal.

INTEGRATOR OF MUSICAL STYLES

Elvis Presley was a white man, but he did not sing like most white singers of his time. From childhood on, he loved gospel, R&B, and country—types of music that were not generally appreciated by middle-class white Americans. Later, when he became popular, Elvis essentially reached across an invisible "color line" by incorporating those sounds into his own music. He brought musical forms like rhythm

and blues out of **segregated** black communities and made them popular with his huge, predominantly white following.

Many black musicians appreciated Elvis's taste in music and the effect it had on white listeners. The famous African-American singer and guitar player B. B. King is among them. He once said, "He's been a shot in the arm to the business, and all I can say is 'that's my man.'"

Discriminatory laws in the South prevented blacks from sharing public waiting areas with whites, as shown at this Texas bus station in 1961.

POP ICON

Kids in the 1950s and 1960s thought that Elvis Presley lived the American dream. In part, that was because he rose from poverty to fame and fortune, seemingly overnight. But Elvis was not just rich. He was also young and sexy. And he had his own style.

Part of his style was the way he dressed and wore his hair. At a time when most singers dressed conservatively, with men wearing jackets and ties, Elvis might have

Female fans screamed with delight when Elvis sang and shook all over, as he did at this 1956 concert.

come onstage wearing colorful and frilly clothing. Eventually, he wore elaborate costumes when he performed. He also grew long sideburns and styled his greased-back hair on top of his head.

Another part of Elvis's style was the way he moved. Unlike most other white performers of the 1950s, he displayed fantastic energy onstage. He wiggled his hips, shook his head, and shuddered all over as he sang and played his guitar. One reviewer commented, "His hips swing sensuously from side to side and his entire body takes on a frantic quiver, as if he had swallowed a jackhammer." Critics and parents did not always like the way Elvis moved (they thought it was too sexy), but young people loved it. He soon earned the nicknames "Swivel Hips" and "Elvis the Pelvis."

By the late 1950s, Elvis Presley defined what was "in" and "cool." Fans all over the world loved his mannerisms, and millions imitated the "Elvis look."

AN ENTERTAINER WITH STAYING POWER

Over the next two decades, Elvis Presley went through periods of lesser and greater popularity. For a few years, in the mid-1960s, he seemed to have faded from the music scene almost entirely. But then, in 1968, Elvis revived his career. He recorded several hit songs, and his concerts sold out everywhere he performed. Elvis Presley continued performing for millions of adoring fans until he died in 1977.

More than twenty-five years have passed since Elvis Presley's death. Nevertheless, he remains extraordinarily popular. Both his songs and his public image continue to inspire songwriters, performers, and fans all over the world. For many people, Elvis Presley is still a trailblazing king.

CHAPTER 2

Elvis Presley's parents, Vernon Presley and Gladys Smith, met at a church function in Tupelo, Mississippi. They married in 1933 and stayed in Tupelo, where both worked at odd jobs. By any standard, the Presleys were poor. When they built their first home, they could not afford either electricity or indoor plumbing.

On January 8, 1935, Gladys gave birth to twin boys at home. She named them Jessie Garon Presley and Elvis Aaron Presley, because she wanted their middle names to rhyme. Elvis's middle name was accidentally misspelled on his birth certificate. From then on, his legal name was Elvis Aron Presley. Jessie died at birth. Soon afterward, Gladys Presley learned that she could have no more children.

Vernon Presley and Gladys Smith Presley posed for a happy portrait in 1948, when Elvis was thirteen years old.

Elvis was born and lived in this tiny house, built next door to his grandfather's home in Tupelo, Mississippi.

A SURPRISING SONG

Elvis Presley's first few years were rather unremarkable. In 1939, when he was four years old, World War II started. In 1941, when he was almost seven, the Japanese bombed Pearl Harbor, and the United States entered the war. The whole world was in turmoil. Nonetheless, life in small-town Mississippi went on, at least for the Presleys. They had very little money, but they got by.

Childhood acquaintances report that Elvis was a very shy child—so shy that if he had not become famous later in life, many might not have remembered him at all.

Few people knew it at the time, but the shy little boy loved music and singing. In 1945, when Elvis was ten years old and the war was ending, his fifth-grade teacher encouraged him to enter a talent contest. The competition was held at the Mississippi-Alabama Fair and Dairy Show, and Elvis's whole class was there on a field trip. To almost everyone's surprise, Elvis agreed to participate. He climbed onto the stage and sang "Old Shep," a **tearjerker** about a boy and his dog. In this, his first public performance, he placed fifth.

Shortly after Elvis sang in the talent show, Vernon and Gladys scraped together enough money to buy him a guitar. A young minister and a kind uncle then taught Elvis a few chords. The preacher also encouraged Elvis to sing in church. The Presleys were members of the Assembly of God church, and they attended services regularly. Elvis loved singing hymns, and he was practically transported by harmonizing in the manner of his favorite gospel quartet, the Blackwood Brothers. And, of course, his minister gave him plenty of encouragement. Elvis knew all the gospel songs by heart but, according to some sources, he would sing only if the minister asked him. According to Elvis, the situation was only slightly different: "I took the guitar, and I watched people, and I learned to play a little bit. But I would never sing in public. I was very shy about it, you know."

Three-year-old Elvis poses for an early photograph that later graced the cover of his 1971 *Elvis Country* album.

Generous Acts

Elvis's guitar was his most treasured possession. By seventh grade, he was even taking it to school almost every day. Once some bullies in the eighth grade cut his guitar strings. Elvis was too poor to replace the strings, but a few friends got together and bought a complete set of strings so he could keep on strumming. Generous acts like that meant a lot to young Elvis. Many years later, when he was rich, he was extraordinarily generous with friends, family, and even complete strangers.

EARLY MUSICAL INFLUENCES

While the Presleys lived in Tupelo, Elvis often listened to a country radio program that was broadcast from the Grand Ole Opry in Nashville, Tennessee. Country music spoke to the young boy, and he wanted to play guitar the way the country musicians did.

Luckily, through a friend at school named James Ausborn, Elvis had a country music connection. That connection was Mississippi Slim, James's brother. Slim hosted a local radio program called *Singin' and Pickin' Hillbilly*, in which he played country music and told jokes. James later recalled that "A lot of people didn't like my brother;

The Grand Ole Opry

In 1925, radio station WSM in Nashville, Tennessee, began broadcasting a live program every Saturday evening. That country music program, *Grand Ole Opry*, was primarily heard in the South and the Midwest. Its name (a spoof of "grand old opera") made fun of its own attempt to be sophisticated.

Country music was anything but refined. This type of music was played on fiddles, guitars, banjos, and accordions. Country humor and storytelling were part of the experience, too. Performing on either the Opry's Saturday program or the *Louisiana Hayride* (a competing program out of Shreveport, Louisiana) could help start a young singer's career.

they thought he was sort of corny, but . . . Elvis would always say, 'Let's go to your brother's program today. . . . I want him to show me more chords on the guitar.'" So Elvis began to learn how to pick and strum his guitar, country-style.

The Presley family moved many times while they lived in Tupelo. At one point they lived near an African-American neighborhood. There, Elvis listened to blues beats and heard black men and women singing **spirituals** when they went to church and attended **revival meetings**. The growing boy soaked up the different rhythms of this music, just as he soaked up country inflections and the gentler beats and harmonies of white church music.

MAMA AND MEMPHIS

Having lost one son, Gladys Presley was not going to risk losing the other. Years later, Presley recalled that his mother was so concerned about his safety that she did not even let him ride a bicycle because she was afraid he might get hit by a car. Young Elvis enjoyed a caring relationship with his parents. Mrs. Presley and Elvis were especially close. Gladys adored him, and he loved her.

To outsiders, it often seemed that the elder Presleys babied Elvis too much. "They treated him like he was two years old," said one neighbor. Even family members commented

Another Childhood Interest

By the time he reached his teens, Elvis was completely hooked on music. According to James Ausborn, "He was crazy about music. That's all he talked about." He may not have talked about anything else, but Elvis did have at least one other interest—comic books. His favorite hero was Captain Marvel. Years later he told a crowd, "When I was a child, . . . I was a dreamer. I read comic books, and I was the hero of the comic book. I saw movies, and I was the hero in the movie."

that Vernon, Gladys, and Elvis Presley were unusually devoted to each other. They spent their free time together and did not socialize much with other people.

Gladys believed that she, her husband, and her son could better themselves. She also believed that they would find more opportunities in Memphis, Tennessee. So, in 1948, the Presleys moved north to Memphis.

When his family moved, Elvis was still crazy about playing the guitar. His new neighbors in Memphis later remembered that he was forever strumming his guitar and singing to himself while sitting on the steps of the family's apartment. An older boy who lived in the same public housing project had a similar interest, and he taught Elvis a few more chords and techniques.

Neither of Elvis's parents had finished high school, and Gladys Presley always wanted her son to get his

By 1945, the close-knit family had moved several times within Tupelo so Vernon and Gladys could find work and affordable housing.

Who Are You Calling "Trash"?

The Presley family lived in Tupelo until Elvis was thirteen years old. Even then, his family was still poor. Other people sometimes looked down on the Presleys as "trash." Elvis and his parents hated that term because it implied that they were not just poor but also ignorant and lazy. Vernon later said: *There were times we had nothing to eat but corn bread and water, but we always had compassion for people. Poor we were, I'll never deny that. But trash we weren't. . . . We never had any prejudice. We never put anybody down. Neither did Elvis.*

Activities: F. H. A., History Club, English Club, Vice-President History Club.

RULEMAN, SHIRLEY

Major: Home Ec., Commercial, English.
Activities: National Honor Society, F. H. A., Y-Teens, Latin Club, Jr. Cheerleader, Sabre Club, History Club, English Club, Honorary Captain in R. O. T. C., President Home Ec. Class.

PRESLEY, ELVIS ARON

Major: Shop, History, English.
Activities: R. O. T. C., Biology Club, English Club, History Club, Speech Club.

Elvis's Hume High School yearbook entry in 1953 provides no clues to his musical interest or talent.

diploma. Elvis stayed in school and did well enough to get by. Years afterwards, he recalled, "I failed music—only thing I ever failed." He continued to be a quiet, polite, and respectful boy, but he was not very popular with his classmates.

Elvis Presley fulfilled his mother's wish by graduating from Hume High School in 1953. By then, he knew that his parents had sacrificed a great deal for him, and he wanted to repay them. According to his senior prom date, his biggest dream was to get "a job so he could buy a house for his mama."

Elvis did get a job. He was soon driving a truck for an electrical contracting company, and Gladys Presley was very pleased. Little did she and Vernon know that being a truck driver was not enough for their son. What Elvis really wanted was to be a singer.

The Guitar Man

In 1953, Elvis appeared as the "Guitar Man" in the annual Hume High School talent show. He was so self-conscious that he did not tell his parents or his girlfriend that he intended to perform. "When I came onstage," he later said, "I heard people kind of rumbling and whispering and so forth, 'cause nobody knew I even sang." He added, "It was amazing how popular I became after that."

THE MAKING OF A POP IDOL

It was a summer day in Memphis in 1953. Sun Records, owned by Sam Phillips, had a sign in the window. "Make your own records," it said. "Four dollars for two songs." A nervous eighteen-year-old walked through the door. He had four dollars, a guitar, and no shortage of songs.

Something about the boy caught the eye of studio assistant and Memphis radio personality Marion Keisker. She asked about his singing style. Elvis Presley replied, "I don't sing like nobody."

Elvis recorded two songs that day. Both were by the Ink Spots, a black quartet whose music often had a rhythm-and-blues feel. Sam Phillips listened as the songs were recorded. Then Elvis paid for his record and left.

Holding a stack of his first 45 rpm record, Elvis is captured in a casual moment.

Ten months later, on July 5, 1954, Elvis was back at Sun Records. This time he was with two Sun Studio regulars, guitarist Scotty Moore and bass player Bill Black. They were in the studio not as paying customers, but to audition for Sam Phillips.

The three men played several tunes for Phillips. He was not especially impressed and told the musicians to take a break. As they relaxed, Elvis fooled around with his guitar. Slapping its back, he sang, "That's All Right," a tune made famous by African-

Elvis Presley, bassist Bill Black, and guitarist Scotty Moore in 1954, at the Sun Records studio with Sam Phillips (far right).

Sam Phillips launched the careers of "The Million Dollar Quartet"—Presley, Jerry Lee Lewis, Roy Orbison, and Carl Perkins—by recording them first on Sun Records.

Jerry Lee Lewis, another Sun Records rockabilly discovery, electrified audiences with his wild stage antics.

Sun Records

Sam Phillips started Sun Records in Memphis in 1952. At the time, his new venture seemed impractical—Phillips focused mostly on black musicians, and they did not have a large enough following to bring in a profit. But Phillips believed that he could be successful if he could encourage more white people to listen to rhythm and blues. All he needed was an energetic white singer with a bluesy style and a love for R&B. And that, of course, is what Elvis Presley proved to be.

Elvis was not Sam Phillips' only star. Phillips eventually recorded many legendary singers, such as B. B. King, Howlin' Wolf, Johnny Cash, Jerry Lee Lewis, and Roy Orbison. Because Sun recorded so many talented and influential artists, Sam Phillips is often called the father of rock 'n' roll.

On January 23, 1986, Elvis Presley and Sam Phillips were in the first group of **inductees** to be welcomed into The Rock and Roll Hall of Fame in Cleveland, Ohio.

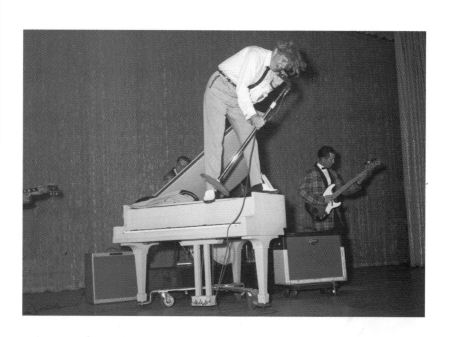

American blues musician Arthur "Big Boy" Crudup. Presley's rocking rendition appealed to Phillips. More enthusiastic now, he called the men back into the studio and asked them to perform the song that same way.

Phillips had a recording of "That's All Right" by the time the session ended. He then took his copy of the song to a local radio station and asked the disc jockey to play it. As a favor to Sam, the DJ agreed to spin the record that evening.

Elvis was so nervous about how the song might be received that he could not bear to listen at home with his parents. Instead, he went to the movies. That evening, Gladys Presley heard the song on the air. In fact, she heard it played seven or eight times in a row. Then she got a call from the jockey. "Mrs. Presley," he said, "you just get that cotton-picking son of yours down here to the station. I played that record of his, and them bird-brain phones haven't stopped ringing since."

EARLY LIVE PERFORMANCES

On July 17, 1954, Elvis, Scotty, and Bill played their first gig at a local club. Days later, they played to a crowd in Memphis' Overland Park. They were amazed by the reception they got. "The first time that I appeared on stage, it scared me to death," Elvis remembered. "I really didn't know what all the yelling was about. I didn't realize that my body was moving. It's a natural thing to me. So to the manager backstage I said, 'What'd I do? What'd I do?' And he said, 'Whatever it is, go back and do it again.'"

Sam Phillips understood that he might have a rising star in his studio. Trying to appeal to a wide southern audience, he asked Elvis to sing a different kind of song for the flip side of "That's All Right."

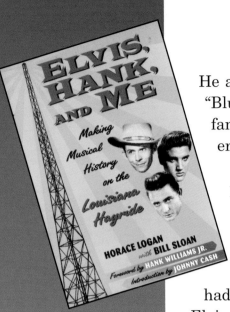

"Hoss" Logan's 1998 book recounts his experience hosting the Shreveport, Louisiana-based radio program that carried Elvis's voice into thousands of southern homes.

Musician Ray Charles blended blues and gospel sounds when he sang, influencing Elvis early in his career.

He asked for an upbeat version of a traditional piece, "Blue Moon of Kentucky." It was a good choice. The familiar lyrics of the song appealed to many southerners, and young people liked its stepped-up tempo. Elvis, Scotty, and Bill started playing on radio programs in the South, and they kept on recording for Sun. By the end of 1955, they had made five records. The band had also performed in dozens of concerts from New Mexico to Florida. And a radio program called *The Louisiana Hayride* had signed the trio to a weekly performance contract. Elvis was paid $18.00 for each radio appearance.

ELVIS AND THE NEW SOUND

In the 1950s, many teenagers wanted a musical sound they could call their own. They were not interested in the Big Band orchestras, quiet jazz combos, and straight-laced singers that appealed to their parents. They wanted to move to music, so they wanted music that really moved.

Elvis Presley gave restless young people the music they wanted. His songs had a strong beat and a gritty feel that made young people want to dance. And his style did not fit into the standard musical categories of the time. He played and sang in many styles—country, R&B,

Blues Influence

In 1956, Elvis talked about blues influences on his music:

The colored folks been singing it and playing it just like I'm doin' now, man, for more years than I know. . . . Down in Tupelo, Mississippi, I used to hear old Arthur Crudup bang his box the way I do now, and I said if I ever got to the place where I could feel all old Arthur felt, I'd be a music man like nobody ever saw.

gospel, and more. Furthermore—and this was even more exciting—he blended those styles into a hot new sound. Thousands of kids who heard him could not get enough.

Many music promoters did not entirely understand what was happening. They were not sure what to call this new sound or how to market Elvis. They tried different labels. First, people said that Elvis was a country singer. Then they called his music **rockabilly**—a blend of country (sometimes called "hillbilly") and R&B. A short while later, at about the time Elvis broke into the pop charts, radio disc jockeys came up with another label. They called the new sound rock 'n' roll.

Elvis and "Race Music"

In the 1950s, many white adults considered African-American music—then called "race music"—to be a bad influence on their children. Rufus Thomas, a prominent black R&B performer, remembered those days: "The white families didn't want their kids to listen to [rhythm and blues]. [The kids] would go to bed at night and put that little radio up under their pillow and listen straight on through." Teens, including Elvis, rocked to the sounds of Little Richard, Chuck Berry, Bo Didley, and other musicians they heard on Memphis' black radio station. Elvis blended these styles to create his own sound.

IN THE SPOTLIGHT

In 1955, Elvis made two important career moves. First, he hired "Colonel" Tom A. Parker to be his manager. "The Colonel" was an experienced marketer who knew how to plan the career of a rising star. The other important move came from Sam Phillips. He sold Elvis Presley's recording contract and all his Sun recordings to RCA/Victor Records, a major recording company that distributed its products all over the United States.

National success quickly followed. Elvis's first release for RCA, "Heartbreak Hotel,"

Elvis's lifelong personal manager, Tom A. Parker, was a former circus promoter and dog catcher before he represented musicians. Parker adopted the honorary title "colonel" to lend him an air of respectability.

Other Early Rockers

Elvis, Scotty, and Bill were not the only people playing rock 'n' roll. In fact, the first all-white band to record this new sound was Bill Haley and the Comets. Their song "Rock Around The Clock" became a huge hit when it was used in the soundtrack of the 1955 movie *The Blackboard Jungle.* Another hot group was Buddy Holly and the Crickets.

They came along shortly after Elvis and had hits with songs like "Peggy Sue." But most of the early rockers agreed that one man was primarily responsible for putting rock 'n' roll on the map. According to Buddy Holly, "Without Elvis, none of us would have made it."

In 1955, Elvis was thrilled to be on the same program in Cleveland, Ohio, with one of his favorite groups, Bill Haley (center) and the Comets.

Elvis was only twenty-one years old when his first album sold over 300,000 copies and rode at the top of the charts for ten weeks.

went to number one on the charts. His second single, "Hound Dog," did the same. The hits kept coming, and Elvis Presley's first four albums for RCA/Victor became number one bestsellers.

After "Heartbreak Hotel," it seemed that everyone took notice of Elvis. Fans and some critics loved him. Other critics and many conservative adults did not. In fact, some of them were antagonistic. Frank Sinatra, the leading recording artist of the time, once declared, "His kind of music is deplorable. . . . It fosters almost totally negative and destructive reactions in young people."

For people who did not approve of him, Elvis Presley's music was not the only problem. He wore surprisingly unusual clothes. And he acted outrageously —thrusting his hips, jiggling and jerking, flirting with girls in the audience, and behaving crudely. Sometimes he even spit his chewing gum into the crowd.

For his fans, this behavior was exciting. For many others (especially conservative adults), it was too much. Elvis Presley was too sexy, too obscene, and too dangerous for impressionable young people to watch.

MEDIA DARLING

As soon as Elvis's records hit the charts, television producers wanted to sign him up for their shows. That was fine with Elvis and the Colonel—TV could help them reach a bigger audience. So, in 1956, the hot young star performed on live TV eleven times.

ELVIS AND ED SULLIVAN

Ed Sullivan's *Toast of the Town* was the most popular variety show of the day. Appalled by Elvis Presley's "swivel hips," Sullivan had publicly announced that audiences would never see him on the program. By September 1956, however, the famous host had to back down. Elvis Presley was simply too popular to pass up. Over the next five months, he appeared three times on Sullivan's show.

The Jordanaires sang back up for Elvis when he appeared for the second time on *Toast of the Town*, in October 1956.

Working with Elvis, Mr. Sullivan got to know him. He saw that behind the wild stage **persona** was a sincere, polite human being. During his last appearance on the show, Elvis even sang a spiritual, "Peaceful Valley," at Sullivan's request. Ed Sullivan then publicly retracted his earlier remarks: "I wanted to say to Elvis Presley and the country that this is a real decent, fine boy."

The outcry against Elvis continued, however, and some comments were quite harsh. When asked about them, he did not react angrily. Instead, he explained, "I don't feel like I'm doing anything wrong. I don't see

Careful Filming

Although Sullivan came to like Elvis, many TV viewers complained that the way he moved was obscene. Finally, prior to Elvis's appearance on the show in January 1957, Sullivan's producers decided to pacify the complainers. That night they ordered the TV cameramen to film Presley only from the waist up. As a result, viewers who watched that week's program never once saw the infamous hips of "Elvis the Pelvis."

how any type of music would have any bad influence on people when it's only music. . . . I mean, how would rock 'n' roll music make anyone rebel against their parents?"

MOVIES, MOVIES, MOVIES

In 1956, Elvis made his first Hollywood movie, a Western-style drama called *Love Me Tender*. The title song was also released as a single. Both the movie and the record were wildly successful. Elvis's first attempt at acting had another important result: movie critics said that his performance was better than expected. That meant a lot to Elvis. He hoped it would lead to more offers of serious acting roles.

For the Colonel, however, acting was not an end in itself. He knew that if Elvis sang in every movie and then released an album when each picture came out, record sales would be phenomenal.

ONE NEW HOME AND THEN ANOTHER

In 1956, when he was only twenty-one years old, Elvis made his high school dream come true—he bought a

Starring Elvis Presley

Elvis Presley acted in thirty-one movies. Here are a few of the most popular.

1956, *Love Me Tender*

1957, *Jailhouse Rock*

1958, *King Creole*

1960, *GI Blues*

1964, *Viva Las Vegas*

1964, *Roustabout*

1966, *Spinout*

house for his parents. Over the next few months, however, it became clear that their new home was too small. Elvis had hired friends and relatives to act as his security guards, and the house could not contain the growing group.

Elvis was making about $100,000 per month at that time, so he could easily afford a larger house. He soon found the perfect place. Called Graceland, it was located on almost 14 acres (6 h) of land in Memphis. It was by far the most beautiful house Elvis and his parents had ever seen. Elvis loved it, and it remained his home for the rest of his life.

This memorable dance sequence from *Jailhouse Rock* made the movie and the song huge hits.

Gladys Presley's beloved 1955 pink Cadillac is shown here parked in front of Graceland, Presley's majestic mansion.

ARMY YEARS

Elvis's acting and singing career was interrupted in 1958 when the U.S. government

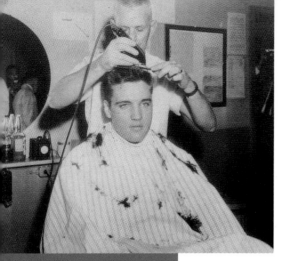

Female fans wept when they saw Elvis's long hair clipped by an army barber in 1958.

Vernon, Gladys, and Elvis Presley pose for a final family portrait before Elvis is shipped overseas in 1958.

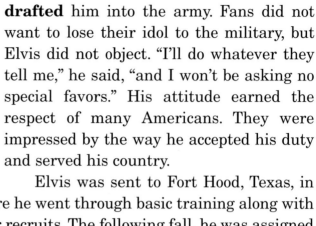

drafted him into the army. Fans did not want to lose their idol to the military, but Elvis did not object. "I'll do whatever they tell me," he said, "and I won't be asking no special favors." His attitude earned the respect of many Americans. They were impressed by the way he accepted his duty and served his country.

Elvis was sent to Fort Hood, Texas, in March. There he went through basic training along with all the other recruits. The following fall, he was assigned to a military base in Germany. Once overseas, Private Presley became an expert marksman, earned a reputation as a shrewd planner of tank maneuvers, and learned karate. He was also promoted to sergeant.

While he was in the army, Elvis did not perform publicly or make records. It was quite a change for him. He missed his fans, and they missed him—he received over ten thousand pieces of fan mail each week.

Elvis's mother died in 1958, and being in the army became even lonelier for him. Elvis missed his mother, Memphis, and his friends. And he missed the way of life he had known. To ease his homesickness, Elvis brought his father, grandmother, and two friends to Germany, where they all shared a house.

Elvis made many new friends abroad. One of them was Priscilla Beaulieu, the daughter of an air force captain. Although she was fourteen and he was twenty-four, Elvis felt that he could be himself with Priscilla. With other people, he felt he had a role to play—either as a rock star or an army private. When he began spending his time with such a young girl, however, there was a good deal of gossip.

A Death in the Family

During the mid-1950s, Gladys Presley was not in good health. She and Elvis were still very close, and her son worried about her often. Whenever he was away from home while touring or making movies, he called her every night.

They were so close that Elvis moved his mother and father into a rental home near Fort Hood. When Gladys became ill in the summer of 1958, however, Elvis sent her back to Memphis to see their family doctor. Her condition soon worsened, and Elvis was granted an emergency leave to visit her in the hospital. His mother died on August 14, 1958, shortly after Elvis arrived. She was forty-six years old.

Her son was filled with grief. At one point Elvis cried, "She's all we lived for. She was always my best girl."

HOME AGAIN

Elvis was released from the army in March 1960. Upon his return to the United States, he was honored in a TV special hosted by singer Frank Sinatra—the man who had once been so critical of him. This "welcome home" event helped put Elvis back in the American spotlight.

Elvis returned to his old career. Under the Colonel's guidance, he acted in as many as four movies and recorded two or three albums each year. And the hits kept coming. In fact, he had four back-to-back number one hits between March 1960 and February 1962. Few entertainers in the early sixties worked as hard or made as much money as Elvis Presley.

Now in his mid-twenties, the star sometimes had trouble maintaining his hectic schedule. He had started taking prescription drugs in Germany. He continued to rely on them now for his work in Hollywood. He took pills to keep him awake and pills to help him sleep.

Frank Sinatra and Elvis Presley sang each other's hit tunes in a 1960 TV special, in which Presley was paid $125,000 for six minutes on screen.

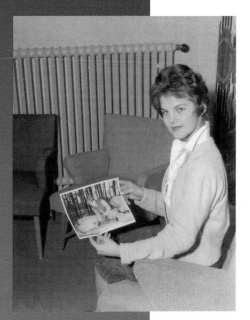

Sixteen-year-old Priscilla Beaulieu looked older than her age in 1960, but her youth was a cause for concern to her parents and the public.

Meanwhile, he kept in touch with Priscilla Beaulieu, who was still overseas. They wrote and talked on the phone often for the first two years. Then, in 1963, she moved to Memphis, where she completed her high school education.

CAREER SLUMP

As the year 1964 began, Elvis was working hard and making huge amounts of money. Unfortunately, his work was no longer as challenging and enjoyable as it had been just a few years before. One Elvis movie was much like the next, and he was not offered the serious dramatic roles he wanted. The songs that were created for his movies were a disappointment, too. They were not the solid R&B material he truly loved.

That year, a new kind of rock 'n' roll took hold in the United States. Called the "British Invasion," it thrust groups like The Beatles, the Dave Clark Five, and the Rolling Stones into the spotlight. Teens everywhere screamed for these new performers, just as they had screamed for Elvis eight years earlier.

In 1962, Elvis's single "Return to Sender" had sold a million copies. Since then, however, his records had not sold as well as expected. Movie attendance was down, too. Audiences seemed to be losing interest. Many people thought that Elvis Presley had become a slick performer without much depth.

BACK TO BASICS

CHAPTER 5

Mr. and Mrs. Elvis Presley

On May 1, 1967, Elvis married Priscilla Beaulieu after an eight-year courtship. Their only child, Lisa Marie Presley, was born nine months later. By the time his daughter was born, Elvis had not had a number one hit single in six years and had not performed publicly in seven years.

By 1967, the social and political climate of the country was changing significantly. American soldiers were dying in Vietnam. At home, people were protesting against the war and in support of **civil rights legislation**. Singers like Bob Dylan, Joan Baez, and Peter, Paul & Mary inspired the protesters with their antiwar, **antiestablishment** songs. Elvis Presley's music lagged behind the times.

The year 1968 was even more turbulent. In April, the distinguished civil rights leader, Dr. Martin Luther King Jr., was slain. Three months later, Robert F.

Priscilla Beaulieu and Elvis were married in Las Vegas, Nevada, at the Aladdin hotel in a morning ceremony.

The National Guard restored order in Washington, D.C., when riots broke out in response to the assassination of Martin Luther King Jr. in 1968.

Kennedy, a respected senator who was running for president, was also murdered. Millions of citizens expressed their grief and anger over the assassinations. Riots broke out in African-American neighborhoods after Dr. King's murder. More than two dozen people died in the violence.

THE "COMEBACK SPECIAL"

While the nation was still reeling from those events, Elvis Presley starred in a TV special. Viewers did not expect much. After all, his movies were predictable, and he had not performed for a live audience in nearly eight years. At the end of the show, however, Elvis did something no one expected: He performed a song whose powerful lyrics echoed the commitment to unity, hope, and racial equality that Dr. King and Senator Kennedy had shared.

Singing to a TV audience, a leather-clad Elvis exudes the sexy showmanship that forever won him the adoration of millions of fans.

Powerful Singer, Powerful Song

"If I Can Dream," by W. Earl Brown, was the song Elvis sang to such effect on his "Comeback Special." Here is the refrain:

If I can dream of a better land
Where all my brothers walk hand in hand
Tell me why, oh why, oh why can't my dream come true

The audience was stunned. Both his choice of the song and the way he sang it changed people's perceptions of Elvis. According to reviewer John Landau, "There is something magical about watching a man who has lost himself find his way back home. . . .

He sang with the kind of power people no longer expect from rock 'n' roll singers." Elvis Presley was not a lightweight or a has-been. He was a man of deep feeling who had something to say and knew how to say it.

After the performance, Elvis spoke with his producers. "I'll never sing another song that I don't believe in," he told them. "I'm never going to make another movie that I don't believe in."

Elvis Presley's December 1968 TV show soon became known as his "Comeback Special."

Elvis introduced a flashy, Las Vegas fashion style, wearing studded jumpsuits and silk scarves and carrying his guitar merely as an accessory.

ON TOP AGAIN

In August 1969, Elvis performed live in Las Vegas, Nevada. The press gave him rave reviews, and audiences fell in love with "The King" all over again. After Las Vegas, he began touring to other cities. He started conservatively, booking just a few gigs to test audience response.

The response was wildly enthusiastic. Audiences loved Elvis's sparkling new look, which usually consisted of studded and sequined jumpsuits with matching capes. They also loved the way Elvis seemed to feed off their enthusiasm. He even incorporated karate into his high-powered performances, giving expert demonstrations between songs.

For both his concerts and his albums, Elvis now returned to his greatest strength—expressing emotion through song. He added different types of songs (gospels, hymns, and ballads) that highlighted this natural talent. A few of the new songs were big hits, including "Suspicious Minds," his first single to reach number one since "Good Luck Charm" in 1962. "In the Ghetto" and "Don't Cry, Daddy" also made the top ten in 1969 and early 1970. Both songs told painful stories in a touching, troubling way that many listeners appreciated.

Elvis Presley was once again a tremendously successful entertainer and singer. Frank Lieberman of the *Herald-Examiner* even predicted that "the new decade [the 1970s] will belong to him."

BAD GUYS, GOOD GUYS

Elvis expanded his tours. While he was on the road, he often hired local policemen as extra security. Elvis Presley was such a huge superstar that many policemen were surprised to find that he was not arrogant. They liked Elvis, and, to their surprise and pleasure, he liked them.

Elvis began attending the policemen's weddings and funerals. He also donated money to their charities. Many officers appreciated Elvis's genuine interest in their profession. Some even gave him official deputy and sheriff badges as thanks. Elvis was thrilled and honored. He carried the badges with him and proudly displayed them whenever he got the chance.

In the early 1970s, drugs and drug-related crime were already big problems. Elvis wanted to help police departments catch the offenders. He somehow became convinced that he could go undercover and help find and arrest drug dealers. He even wrote a letter to President Richard M. Nixon in which he offered to do just that. The president responded by inviting Elvis to the White House.

The two met on December 21, 1970. That day, the president gave Elvis Presley a badge and made him an honorary undercover officer for the Bureau of Narcotics and Dangerous Drugs (BNDD) at the Federal Bureau of Investigation (FBI). It was one of Elvis Presley's proudest moments. Many of his fans, disturbed by growing drug use among young people, supported Presley's gesture. Others felt it was a **publicity stunt** and questioned his **motives**.

Sadly, there was a darker side to Elvis Presley's involvement with drugs. Despite his outward show of support for antidrug activities and his publicity photos with Nixon, Elvis had a serious drug problem of his own. Because it involved prescription drugs, however, it did

Elvis wore a velvet cape and his "championship" gold belt when meeting with President Richard M. Nixon in the Oval Office in 1970.

not receive the attention it would have if the drugs had been illegal. Elvis had been taking both painkillers and sleeping pills for a long time and took them every day. Many of the people in his inner circle knew he was addicted to prescription drugs. Unfortunately, no one—friends, family, or police buddies—could make him see that he needed treatment. Elvis was headed for trouble.

From "The King" to The President

In December 1970, while flying to Washington, D.C., Elvis wrote this note to President Richard M. Nixon.

Dear Mr. President:

First, I would like to introduce myself. I am Elvis Presley and admire you and have great respect for your office. I talked to Vice President Agnew in Palm Springs three weeks ago and expressed my concern for our country.

The drug Culture, the hippie elements, . . . do not consider me as their enemy. . . . Sir, I can and will be of any service that I can to help the country out. . . .

I can and will do more good if I were made a Federal Agent at Large and I will help out by doing it my way through communications with people of all ages. First and foremost, I am an entertainer, but all I need is the federal credentials. . . .

I have done an in-depth study of drug Abuse . . . and I am right in the middle of the whole thing where I can and will do the most good. I am glad to help just so long as it is kept very private. . . .

I would love to meet you just to say hello if you're not too busy. . . .

Respectfully,
Elvis Presley

"The King" seemed to be on top of the world in the early 1970s. His concerts sold out; his albums did well; and he loved the excitement of performing for a live audience.

A Treasured Award

In January 1971, the United States Junior Chamber of Commerce (the JayCees), an organization of business leaders, honored Elvis Presley as one of 1970's "Ten Outstanding Young Men of the Year." The citation praised his "strength of character, his loyalty to his friends," and his charitable acts.

Elvis had received awards in the past and would receive more in the future—Grammies, special achievement awards, and even a Lifetime Achievement Award from the National Academy of Recording Arts and Sciences. But none meant as much to him as being selected one of the "Ten Outstanding Young Men of the Year."

ON A ROLL

In June 1972, Elvis Presley became the first entertainer to sell out Madison Square Garden concerts four days in a row. RCA released *Elvis as Recorded at Madison Square Garden* just days later. Within two months, the album sold enough copies to become a gold record. It was Elvis's bestselling album in nine years and reached number eight on the pop charts.

Taking Care of Business

After his comeback, Elvis put together a new band. He named it TCB, which was short for "taking care of business." Elvis thought of himself as someone who took care of business in a flash—like a lightning bolt. One night, he designed a logo by writing the letters TCB and adding a lightning bolt. He sent the design to his personal jeweler for use in rings and pendants. Elvis later gave that special jewelry to band members and friends.

On January 14, 1973, Elvis gave a charity concert in Hawaii. It was a huge musical, technical, and fundraising effort and an enormous success. The live concert was seen first in Asia, then (via tape-delay technology) in Europe, then, three months later, in the United States. RCA/Victor quickly cut and released *Elvis, Aloha from Hawaii via Satellite*, an album that zoomed to the top of the charts and became the number-one album of 1973.

COMING APART

Between 1970 and 1977, Elvis performed in more than one thousand concerts across the United States. He also spent more money, buying three private jets, dozens of cars, jewelry for his band and back-up singers, and a new home in Beverly Hills, California. In one two-day shopping spree, he bought and gave away $85,000 worth of jewelry.

The superstar lifestyle certainly had its rewards, but it did not help Elvis avoid or solve personal problems. During the early 1970s, his marriage was in trouble. He was also abusing drugs, and he gained weight by eating too much junk food (including deep-fried peanut butter and mashed banana sandwiches). As he reflected at one press conference, "Well, the image is one thing and the human being another. It's very hard to live up to an image."

The lifestyle became too much for Priscilla Presley. She later commented, "I felt that I just couldn't reach him anymore. He had bought his own image, and you couldn't have [a real] conversation with him. . . . I think deep down he wanted to be a family man. But he was serving too many masters." Priscilla left her husband in 1972 and divorced him on October 9, 1973.

Priscilla and Elvis called quits to their marriage in 1973, when she was 26 and he was 38.

Depressed and lonely after the divorce, Elvis withdrew. He saw only the "Memphis Mafia" (his inner circle of male friends), family, and a parade of girlfriends. He was hospitalized several times during this period, twice for serious drug-related illnesses. "The King" was tired and out of shape.

THE DECLINE

Even though he was exhausted, Elvis was spending so much money that he had to work more to pay his bills. To keep going, he took even

Elvis Helps Out

Elvis Presley was a very generous man. When his record producer needed a kidney transplant, for example, Elvis paid for the operation. He also helped pay the medical bills of two of his R&B inspirations, Jackie Wilson and Ivory Joe Hunter. To friends, he gave jewelry, cars, and horses, and he sometimes paid for their weddings and homes. He was equally generous to strangers. If you were in a car showroom the day Elvis was there, he might buy you the Cadillac of your dreams!

He made big contributions to charitable organizations, too. Each Christmas, he donated at least $1,000 each to fifty charities in Memphis. He also gave freely and often to emergency relief programs. Hundreds of families whose lives had been devastated by storms never knew that Elvis Presley had donated their replacement mobile homes.

Elvis gave his first charity concert in Honolulu in 1961. That benefit raised $65,000 to help build a memorial to those who died when Japanese forces attacked Pearl Harbor in 1945. And his 1973 concert, Aloha! From Hawaii, raised $75,000 for a cancer fund.

Overweight, puffy eyed, and at times disoriented, Elvis fell victim to his superstar lifestyle.

more pills, which affected both his moods and his health. Between 1972 and 1976, he was unable to complete several shows because of health issues.

By 1976, many of Elvis's performances were sloppy. His speech was sometimes slurred; he often forgot the words to his songs; and he was unsteady on stage. A Houston critic who saw a 1976 performance wrote, "Elvis Presley has been breaking hearts for more than twenty years now, and . . . in a completely new and unexpected way, he broke mine." The show, he continued, was "a depressingly incoherent, amateurish mess served up by a bloated, stumbling and mumbling figure who didn't act like 'The King' of anything, least of all rock 'n' roll."

Bursting out of his "Aztec Sun" jumpsuit, Elvis performed before 14,000 fans in Providence, Rhode Island, just months before his death.

"THE KING" HAS FALLEN

Elvis Presley continued touring in 1977, even though he was suffering from intestinal and eye problems that needed constant medical attention. Before the first of July that year, he gave fifty-four concert performances. He finished in Indianapolis, Indiana with what many felt was his best concert in a long time. Before leaving, he turned to the crowd and said, "Till we meet you again, may God bless you. Adios." He departed for Memphis, where he hoped to relax before starting his next tour on August 17.

On August 16, 1977, after a late night game of racquetball, Elvis told his fiancée, Ginger Alden, that he could not sleep and was going to the bathroom to read. Many hours later, she found him slumped over. Attempts to revive him were unsuccessful—he was dead. Elvis Presley was only forty-two years old.

Doctors announced that the cause of death was a heart attack. Many have speculated, however, that his death was due to years of drug abuse.

People all around the world grieved, and over one hundred thousand went to Memphis for the funeral. Elvis was buried near his mother in Forest Hill Cemetery in Memphis as grieving fans mobbed the streets and said prayers near Graceland.

A few months later, Vernon Presley received permission to move the graves of Gladys Smith Presley and Elvis Aron Presley. Their remains now rest in the meditation garden at Graceland.

On August 17, 1977, Graceland was opened to the public for the first time so fans could view the body of Elvis Presley.

LONG LIVE "THE KING"

CHAPTER 7

Elvis Presley died more than twenty-five years ago, but he remains famous. Some people have even suggested that his death brought his career back to life. Each year on the anniversary of his death, fans gather in Memphis for a nine-day event known as "Elvis Week." On August 16, 2002, the twenty-fifth anniversary of his death, thirty-five thousand people attended a memorial prayer service and visited Presley's grave. Another seventy-five thousand attended a sold-out arena show, "Elvis, The Concert World Tour."

Books and articles about Elvis continue to be published, and legends have sprung up. Some of the most interesting stories claim that Elvis is still alive. Over the years, **tabloids** have often announced that "The King"

Fans pay respect to Elvis in Graceland's Meditation Garden on the twenty-fifth anniversary of Presley's death, August 16, 2002.

has been spotted in a grocery store, a trailer park, or some other ordinary place. Even more imaginative tales say that Elvis was abducted by aliens and taken to another planet.

PASSING THE BUCK

Elvis Presley's estate has become a big business. At first, however, it was worth little. Even though he was the highest paid entertainer of his time, Elvis spent or gave most of his money away. There was not much left when he died.

Lisa Marie Presley married her third husband, actor Nicolas Cage, in August 2002, just days before attending the twenty-fifth anniversary ceremonies for her father in Memphis.

Elvis's father, Vernon, and his ex-wife, Priscilla, greatly increased the wealth of his estate through careful management of Elvis Presley's image and music. Vernon Presley died in 1979 at the age of sixty-three. In 1993, Elvis's daughter, Lisa Marie Presley, inherited the estate and became the sole owner of Elvis Presley Enterprises. She has since formed the Elvis Presley Charitable Trust, which donates money to charitable causes.

Thanks to the efforts of Vernon, Priscilla, and Lisa Marie Presley, Elvis's estate earned $37 million in 2001. Most of the money came from sales of his music and licensing of his name and image for products. It made Elvis Presley the top-earning dead celebrity of 2001.

MUSICAL HIGH NOTES

Sales of Elvis Presley's recordings continue to break American industry records. In its last tally, RCA counted eighty-four gold, forty-five platinum, and twenty-one

Graceland's racquetball room is decorated with Presley's gold and platinum records as well as some of his favorite stage costumes.

A Visit to Graceland

Built in 1939 by a Memphis doctor, Graceland was sold to Elvis Presley for $100,000 in 1957. The estate provided much-needed privacy for the superstar and his parents, and it remained Elvis's home for twenty years.

In 1982, Graceland opened as a museum. More than six hundred thousand fans make the pilgrimage there each year. Tours of Graceland include rooms where Elvis played pool, watched TV, and recorded music, all still decorated in their original 1960s or 1970s style. Some of Elvis's gold, platinum, and multiplatinum awards are on display as well, as are his costumes, movie souvenirs, gun and badge collection, guitars, and fan mail. Bedrooms of family members are not part of the tours. Tours end in the peaceful meditation garden where Elvis Presley, his parents, and his grandmother are buried. Across the street from Graceland is a part of Elvis's car and motorcycle collection and his airplanes.

multiplatinum records. By some estimates, Elvis's records have sold nearly a billion copies worldwide.

In 2002, a Belgian disc jockey remixed "The King's" 1968 song, "A Little Less Conversation." The remix became the number one seller in Great Britain. With that record, Elvis Presley overtook The Beatles for having the most chart toppers in that country.

Elvis's music continues to be used in movies. One of those movies, *Lilo & Stitch*, was released in 2002. Because its soundtrack featured Elvis Presley singing six songs, the movie helped introduce "The King of Rock 'n' Roll" to a whole new generation of listeners.

In 2002, Priscilla Presley unveiled a new Elvis CD featuring thirty number one hits by her former husband.

So Famous That . . .

When a survey was taken in China and participants were asked to name three westerners, the results were astounding. One of the three people named most often was Elvis Presley. The other two were Richard M. Nixon and Jesus.

President Bill Clinton, a fan of "The King," was given the code name "Elvis" by his Secret Service bodyguards.

The British rocker Declan Patrick MacManus changed his name to Elvis Costello the year Elvis Presley died. He has had a successful recording career ever since.

Thousands of men and women have impersonated Elvis for fun and profit. Each year during Memphis' "Elvis Week," fans look forward to the "Elvis Impersonator" contest.

The United States Postal Service put a 1950s likeness of Elvis on five hundred million first-class stamps in 1993 after asking customers to vote for either a 1950s or 1970s image of Elvis.

A few of the thousands of men (and women) who impersonate "the King" for fun and profit gather in Memphis to honor their idol.

Over one million people voted to put this colorful 1950s portrait of Elvis on a first-class U.S. stamp.

Musicians on Elvis

Before Elvis, there was nothing.
    John Lennon of The Beatles

Elvis had an influence on everybody with his musical approach. He broke the ice for all of us.
    Al Green

Elvis is the greatest cultural force in the twentieth century.
    Leonard Bernstein

. . . It was like he came along and whispered some dream in everybody's ear, and somehow we all dreamed it.
    Bruce Springsteen

Hearing him for the first time was like busting out of jail.
    Bob Dylan

Ask anyone. If it hadn't been for Elvis, I don't know where popular music would be. He was the one that started it all off, and he was definitely the start of it for me.
    Elton John

There was always a great deal of respect for Elvis, especially during his Sun sessions. As a black people, we all knew that.
    Chuck D. of Public Enemy

Elvis Presley's music has had a huge impact on the music-loving public, but perhaps it has had an even greater impact on other musicians. His music has influenced Bob Dylan, the Beatles, Elton John, and many other rock 'n' roll and pop singers.

Writer Lester Bangs summed up Elvis Presley's influence on musicians: "I can guarantee you one thing — we will never again agree on anything as we agreed on Elvis."

On his toes and swinging his hips in 1956, Elvis rode a tidal wave that carried rock 'n' roll into the future.

TIMELINE

1935	Elvis Aron Presley is born in Tupelo, Mississippi, on January 8
1948	Moves with his family to Memphis, Tennessee
1954	Makes his first records with Scotty Moore and Bill Black at Sun Records' studios
1955	Stars in his first movie, *Love Me Tender*, which is released the next year
1956	RCA releases his first album, *Elvis Presley*, and it goes to number one
1957	Buys Graceland, which will be his home for twenty years
1958	Enters the army in March; Gladys Smith Presley dies in August
1959	Meets his future wife, Priscilla Beaulieu
1960	Returns to Memphis after being released from the army
1961	Gives a charity concert in Honolulu, Hawaii
1962	*Blue Hawaii* becomes his best-selling album; the movie *Blue Hawaii* reaches number two for the year
1967	Marries Priscilla Beaulieu at the Aladdin Hotel in Las Vegas
1967	Wins "Best Sacred Performance" Grammy for his single "How Great Thou Art"
1968	Lisa Marie Presley is born February 1
1968	Appears in his first television special, *Elvis*, known as the "Comeback Special"
1969	Begins a successful Las Vegas engagement that will become an annual event
1970	Meets President Richard M. Nixon
1971	Receives the Grammy Lifetime Achievement Award
1972	Stars in his last film, a documentary, *Elvis On Tour*
1973	Divorced from Priscilla Beaulieu Presley; hospitalized for problems related to drug abuse
1977	Dies of heart failure on August 16

antiestablishment: against the policies or beliefs of the group of people that is in power

blues: a musical style with lyrics that convey personal suffering or sadness and originated by African Americans

civil rights legislation: laws that eliminate legal segregation and provide equal opportunities for people of all races and backgrounds to vote, work, live, and socialize where they choose

drafted: chosen for government-required service in the armed forces

icon: someone who is the object of great devotion; an idol

inductees: people who have been admitted into a program, service, or membership

motives: reasons for doing something

persona: a person's public image or public personality, as opposed to his or her private life

publicity stunt: an action intended to attract public interest and attention

revival meetings: religious gatherings that feature passionate preaching and energetic praying

rhythm and blues (R&B): a musical style that traditionally combines blues music with black folk music and is marked by a strong beat

rock 'n' roll: a popular music style with a heavy beat that is often played on electronically amplified instruments and is characterized by simple and repeated phrases

rockabilly: popular music that contains elements of both R&B and country music styles

segregated: separated into different neighborhoods, work groups, schools, and public services solely on the basis of race, color, or religion

spirituals: religious songs developed by African Americans in the southern United States

tabloids: newspapers that print sensational headlines and stories in order to attract readers

tearjerker: an extremely sad or pathetic story or song

TO FIND OUT MORE

BOOKS

Denenberg, Barry. *All Shook Up: The Life and Death of Elvis Presley.* New York: Scholastic Trade, 2001.

George-Warren, Holly. *Shake, Rattle and Roll: The Founders of Rock and Roll.* New York: Houghton Mifflin, 2001.

Gordon, Robert. *The Elvis Treasures.* New York: Villard Books, 2002.

Marcovitz, Hal. *Rock 'N' Roll (American Symbols and Their Meanings).* Broomall, Penn.: Mason Crest Publishers, 2002.

Torr, James D. *Elvis Presley.* Farmington Hills, Mich.: Greenhaven Press, 2001.

Woog, Adam. *Rock and Roll Legends.* San Diego: Lucent Books, 2001.

INTERNET SITES

Elvis Presley
www.elvis.com/
Official site of Elvis Presley Enterprises features facts, photographs, virtual tours, and countless bits of information.

Elvis, The Music Never Dies
www.goelvis.com
Features photographs, interactive tours, and stories from past and present articles about "The King," his fans, his hometown, and his music.

Rock and Roll Hall of Fame
www.rockhall.com
Provides biographies on inductees, a timeline, an exhibition gallery, and programs for students.

Recording Industry Association of America
www.riaa.org
Official site of the organization that tracks gold and platinum recordings. It has information on the basics of copyrights, piracy, webcasting, and freedom of speech.

INDEX

About the Author

Adele Q. Brown is an author with a lifelong interest in pop culture, art, and travel. She has written chapters for books on weather disasters, gardening folklore, and literary aliases. Her recent book, *What A Way To Go, Fabulous Funerals of the Famous and Infamous*, combines biography, pop culture, and history in relating the final stories of innovators such as Elvis Presley and Jim Henson. She has worked in the U.S. Senate, public television, corporate America, and with her husband in his photographic studio. Adele is based in New York City. This book is dedicated to her "rocking" nieces Kimberly Brown, Katrina Nelken, and Jordan Nelken.